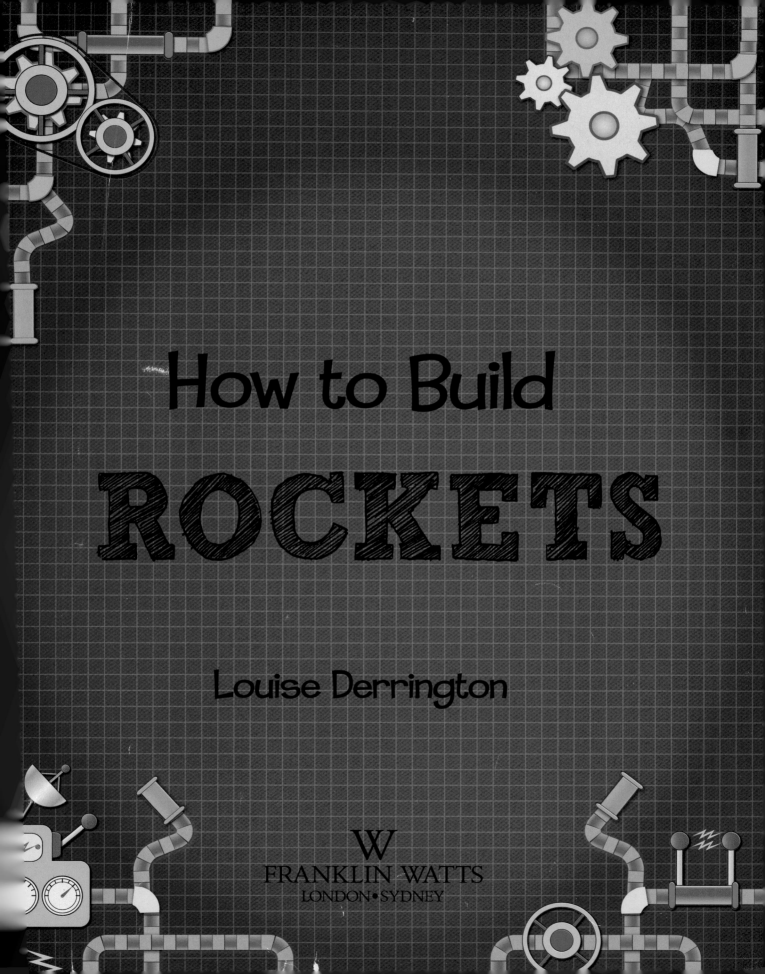

How to Build

ROCKETS

Louise Derrington

W

FRANKLIN WATTS

LONDON • SYDNEY

Franklin Watts
First published in Great Britain in 2016 by
The Watts Publishing Group

Credits
Executive editor: Adrian Cole
Packaged by: Storeybooks
Design manager: Peter Scoulding
Cover design and illustrations: Cathryn Gilbert

Dewey number 621.4'356
ISBN 978 1 4451 4394 1

Printed in China

Photo credits:
The publishers would like to thank the following for permission to reproduce their
pictures: NASA: 4 (middle), 5 (top and bottom), 9, 30 (bottom left, bottom right);
Wikimedia Commons: 4 (top and bottom), 5 (middle), 13, 30 (all except for bottom
left/bottom right).

Step-by-step photography by Tudor Photography, Banbury.

Franklin Watts
An imprint of
Hachette Children's Group
Part of The Watts Publishing Group
Carmelite House
50 Victoria Embankment
London EC4Y 0DZ

An Hachette UK Company
www.hachette.co.uk

www.franklinwatts.co.uk

CONTENTS

SAFETY FIRST
Some of the projects in this book require scissors, sharp tools, fire and matches, a garden fork and wood glue. When using these things we would recommend that children are supervised by a responsible adult.

All about rockets

How did we get from fireworks to space rockets? Although they look very different, they have more in common than you might imagine.

Fireworks were invented by the Chinese many centuries ago. They whizz up into the air when the gunpowder inside them burns, releasing a trail of hot gases that propels them upwards. Space rockets burn rocket fuel rather than gunpowder, but the science is the same.

Payload
A rocket can act as a launch vehicle, carrying a payload. A payload can be a spacecraft containing astronauts or a satellite, or in the case of a military rocket, one or more explosive warheads.

Heavy lifting rockets
Heavy lift launch vehicles are the most powerful type of rocket. They are used to launch satellites and other objects into very high orbits.

The Saturn V rockets used by the National Aeronautics and Space Administration (NASA) were the most powerful heavy lift vehicles ever to have flown successfully. They were used during the Apollo space programme in the 1960s and the 1970s and could launch about 50,000 kg of space rocket into space to reach the Moon. They were capable of lifting even heavier weights – up to 118,000 kg. A Saturn V rocket was used to launch the entire Skylab space station into orbit in 1973, which was the last time a Saturn V rocket flew.

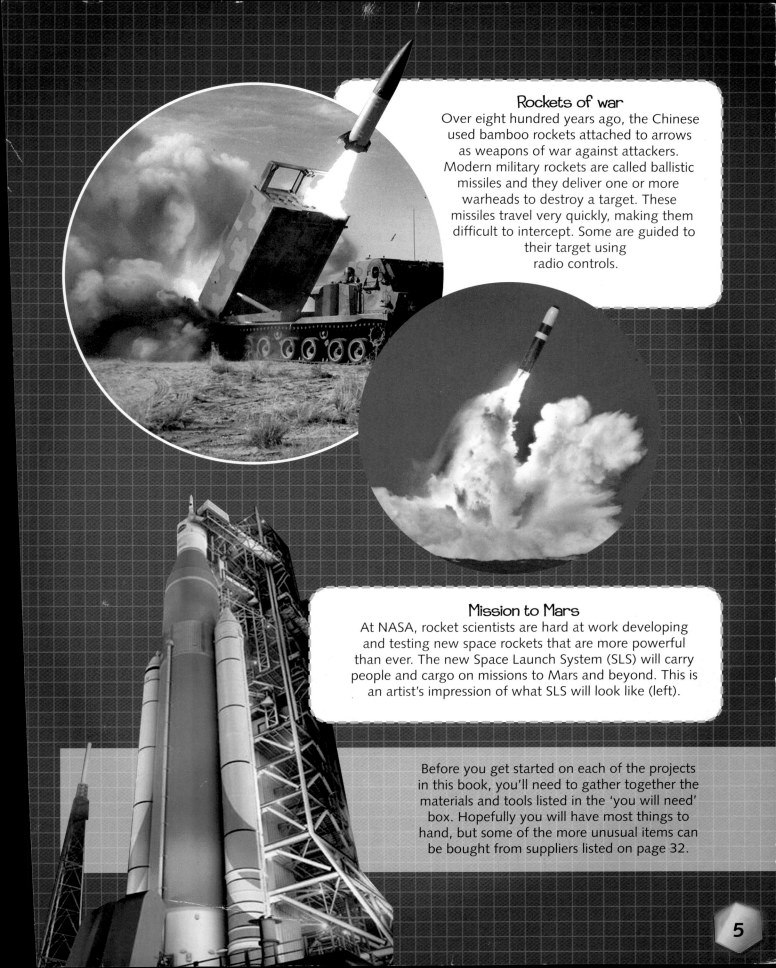

Rockets of war

Over eight hundred years ago, the Chinese used bamboo rockets attached to arrows as weapons of war against attackers. Modern military rockets are called ballistic missiles and they deliver one or more warheads to destroy a target. These missiles travel very quickly, making them difficult to intercept. Some are guided to their target using radio controls.

Mission to Mars

At NASA, rocket scientists are hard at work developing and testing new space rockets that are more powerful than ever. The new Space Launch System (SLS) will carry people and cargo on missions to Mars and beyond. This is an artist's impression of what SLS will look like (left).

Before you get started on each of the projects in this book, you'll need to gather together the materials and tools listed in the 'you will need' box. Hopefully you will have most things to hand, but some of the more unusual items can be bought from suppliers listed on page 32.

Straw rocket

Launch this rocket high into the air with one big blow!

How does it work? The straw rocket will remain still until it is acted on by a force – in this case your breath. When you blow air into the drinking straw, air is forced out of the bottom of the rocket causing it to move through the air in the opposite direction.

To make the straw rocket you will need:
- pencil and thin white paper (for tracing the templates)
- scissors
- A4 sheet thin red card
- A4 sheet thin purple card
- sticky tape
- double-sided tape
- blue sticky tape

1

Use the thin white paper to trace the straw rocket templates on page 28. Use them to cut out one body piece from the red card and two fin pieces and one nose cone from the purple card.

2

Roll the long edge of the red card around the pencil to form a tube. Use sticky tape to fix the edges of the tube together along the length of the tube. Remove the pencil.

3

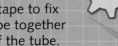

DOUBLE-SIDED TAPE

Stick one length of double-sided tape onto the rectangular part of one fin. Turn the card fin over and bend up the triangular parts of the fin on each side, as shown. Repeat for the other fin.

4

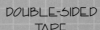

Peel off the backing paper from the double-sided tape on one fin. Stick it to the red card tube, 2 cm from one end. Stick the second fin onto the opposite side of the tube. Looking at your card rocket from the end, the fins should form a cross shape (see below).

CARD TUBE   FIN

5

Wrap a length of blue sticky tape around the card tube, either side of the purple fins. They will hold the fins firmly in place.

Rocket design

When scientists design rockets they are always adapting and improving their ideas. You may have to do the same. All these things listed on the left will make a difference to the way your rocket will fly.

Nose cone The nose cone is the first part of the rocket to push through the air. The length, diameter and position of the nose cone on the rocket will make it more, or less, aerodynamic.

Size (mass) To overcome gravity, the rocket's thrust power needs to be strong enough to lift its weight (mass) up into the air. Model rockets are often made from light materials for this reason. To increase the stability of a model rocket, first find its centre of mass. Balance the rocket on your finger lengthways – the point where it rests on your finger is its centre of mass. To increase the stability of the rocket, add more weight between the centre of mass and the nose cone.

Engines and fuel These are the things that create thrust and propel a rocket. In bottle rockets, the fuel is often water.

Fins The fins on a rocket help it to fly in a straight line. The length, size and position of the fins on a rocket will change the way it flies.

PAYLOAD

THIRD STAGE

SECOND STAGE

FIRST STAGE

Multi-stage rockets

Many space rockets have several stages. As the fuel is used up in the first stage, the empty stage falls back to Earth and the engine in the second stage takes over. This makes the rocket go even faster. When that fuel is used up, this stage is also released and drops back to Earth. The engine in the third stage fires the rocket even higher into space, or into orbit, and then drops away.

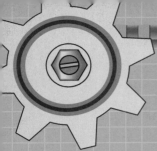

Fizzy rocket

Watch this rocket fizz and fly high into the sky.

How does it work? The fizzy rocket starts to fill up with bubbles of carbon dioxide gas when a chemical reaction starts between the bicarbonate of soda and the vinegar. The bubbles push on the sides of the bottle part of the rocket. Eventually, the pressure builds up so that it pushes the cork out of the bottom of the rocket. The carbon dioxide gas escapes all at once, sending the fizzy rocket shooting up into the air.

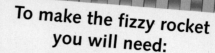

To make the fizzy rocket you will need:
- 500 ml fizzy drink bottle
- duct tape
- 4 x lolly sticks
- ruler
- thin red card
- sticky tape
- pencil and thin white paper (for tracing the templates)
- scissors
- silver card
- star stickers

1

Take the lid off the bottle. Use duct tape to stick the lolly sticks at equal intervals around the bottle opening. Leave 2 cm of the lolly sticks poking out over the bottle top.

2

Cut a piece of red card the same length as the bottle and wide enough to wrap around it with a 1-cm overlap. Wrap the card around the bottle. Tape the edges together to secure them.

3

Use the pencil and white paper to trace the template on page 28 and use it to cut out four fins from the silver card. Bend the flap on each of the fins back at right angles. Tape the flaps on the fins at equal intervals around the rocket body.

4

Trace and cut out the template on page 29 and use it to cut out a nose cone from the silver card. Join the edges of the nose cone so that it fits onto the top of the rocket body and use sticky tape to secure the edges.

5

Tape the cone onto the top of the rocket. Decorate the card with stickers to complete the rocket.

To launch the fizzy rocket you will need:

- safety goggles
- teaspoon
- bicarbonate of soda
- square of kitchen paper
- funnel
- 100 ml white vinegar
- cork that fits the drink bottle opening

SAFETY FIRST

Put on the safety goggles. Launch your fizzy rocket outdoors.

Once you have added the vinegar to the bicarbonate of soda in step 8 you will only have a few minutes to get away from the rocket, so work quickly. Move 10 m back from the fizzy rocket and WAIT. Do NOT be tempted to go and look at the rocket if it doesn't go off. IT WILL – but it may take a couple of minutes.

6

Place a teaspoon of bicarbonate of soda onto a square of kitchen paper.

7

Roll the paper up and twist the ends. Push the twisted kitchen paper inside the bottle part of the rocket.

8

Place the funnel in the bottle opening at the base of the rocket and pour in the white vinegar. Remove the funnel and push in the cork. Give everything a shake.

Act quickly to stand the rocket up on its lolly-stick legs. Move away from the rocket and watch it blast off from a safe distance of at least 10 m.

Try this!

Launch the rocket again but change the amount of bicarbonate of soda. Did it go higher?

Water rocket

Build up the pressure to launch this water rocket.

How does it work? The water rocket uses two separate sources of energy. The fuel is water and the energy is compressed air. As you pump air into the bottle, the pressure inside builds up, pushing the water down, towards the cork. Eventually, the cork pops out and the water and compressed air flow out in a downward force, pushing the rocket in the opposite direction … and off it goes!

To make this water rocket you will need:
- 2 litre plastic fizzy drink bottle
- scissors
- strip of orange card, 4 cm x 32 cm
- strip of orange card, 8 cm x 32 cm
- sticky tape
- strip of red card, 4 cm x 32 cm
- strip of red card, 2 cm x 32 cm
- pencil and thin white paper (for tracing the template)
- A4 sheet of yellow card
- water • cork that fits the drink bottle opening
- valve from a bicycle tyre's inner tube
- foot pump

1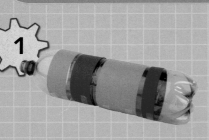

Wrap the narrower strip of orange card around the neck end of the bottle and tape the ends together. Take the wider strip of orange card and repeat, fixing it around the centre of the bottle. Repeat, fixing the red card strips in place, as shown.

2

Use the white paper to trace and cut out the template on page 29 and use it to cut out three fins from the yellow card. Bend back the flap on each of the fins. Stick the flaps at equal intervals around the bottle using sticky tape.

4

Pour water into the bottle until it is a quarter full. Push the cork and valve into the bottle opening to check that it fits. Take it out. Take everything to the launch site.

3

Ask an adult to make a hole through the cork. It needs to be large enough to fit the inner tube valve. Trim the cork so that the valve fits right through it and leave the valve in place.

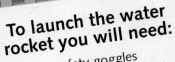

To launch the water rocket you will need:
- safety goggles
- garden fork
- measuring tape
- pencil and paper to record your findings

SAFETY FIRST

Put on safety goggles and launch your rocket outdoors. Safety is very important at any rocket launch. Water rockets are NOT toys. A pressurised water rocket stores huge amounts of energy and flies very fast. IT CAN BURST!
Before you begin, read the full safety code on page 26.

5 Push the garden fork firmly into the ground at an angle of about 45 degrees. Feed the neck of the rocket through the handle of the garden fork and attach the foot pump to the valve in the water rocket's cork. The water rocket should rest on the top of the garden fork facing towards a clear launch area. Start pumping until the cork pops and the rocket blasts off. Use the measuring tape to measure how far the rocket travels. Draw a table to record your findings.

Try these!
Fill the bottle a quarter full.
Fill the bottle half full.
Fill the bottle three-quarters full.
Move the position of the fins.
Add an extra fin.

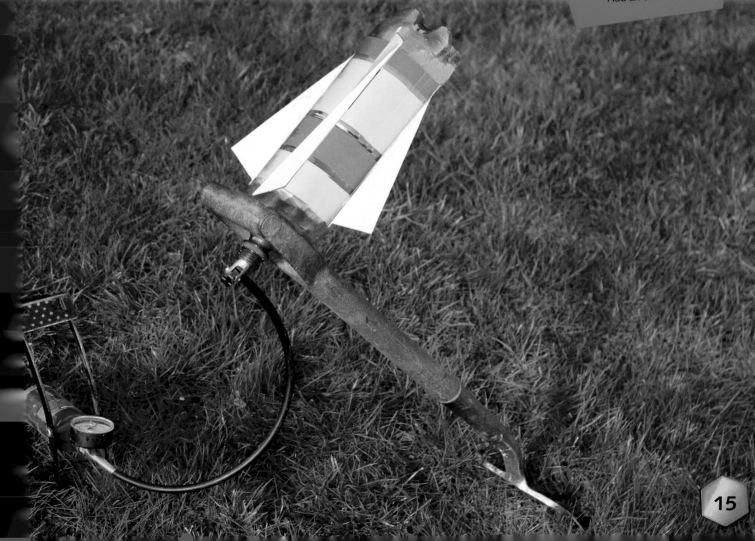

Super water rocket

Launch this rocket and watch it float back down to Earth.

What's going on here? This super water rocket works in the same way as the water rocket on pages 14–15. However, it is bigger, will travel further and it has a parachute in the nose cone. This will give it a softer landing, allowing you to perform repeat launches. Real space rockets use parachutes to help slow the spacecraft down during re-entry and landing.

To make the super water rocket you will need:

- 2 x 2 litre plastic fizzy drink bottles
- scissors • measuring tape
- duct tape
- pencil and thin white paper (for tracing the template)
- A4 sheet of patterned card
- double-sided tape
- table tennis ball, cut in half (ask an adult to do this for you)
- strip of thin red card, 6 cm x 32 cm
- plastic dustbin liner
- ruler • ball of thin string
- 1 m length of thin string
- masking tape • cork
- valve from a bicycle tyre's inner tube
- foot pump

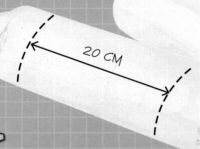

20 CM

1 Carefully cut the top and bottom off one bottle. Keep the top for step 6.

2 Slide the bottom half of this plastic bottle onto the base of the other plastic bottle.

3 Use duct tape to tape the two bottles together.

4 Trace and cut out the template on page 28 and use it to cut out three fins from the printed card. Fold one fin along the two fold lines that meet at (A). Repeat with the other two fins.

A

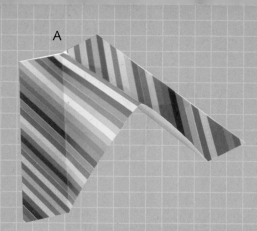

5 Use double-sided tape to stick the fins at equal distances around the bottle. They need to be fixed around the body of the bottle, closest to the bottle's neck. The point of each fin (A) must point away from the neck of the bottle.

A

6

To make the nose cone, take the top of the bottle that you cut off in step 1. Ask an adult to cut off the neck where it becomes straight.

7

Use thin strips of duct tape to tape half a table tennis ball over the hole. Smooth the strips of tape down as much as possible.

8

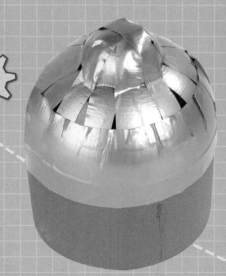

Wrap the strip of red card around the nose cone, and stick it to the nose cone with duct tape.

9

Lay the plastic dustbin liner on a flat surface. Cut off the bottom and along the length of one side in order to leave a large rectangle of plastic. Fold in half.

10

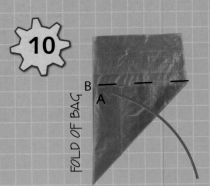

Lay the plastic on a flat surface. Bring corner (A) up to meet point (B). Cut off the top portion of the plastic above the dotted lines.

11

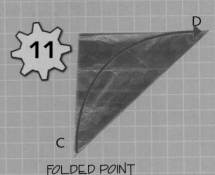

Fold point (C) to meet point (D).

12

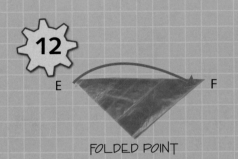

Fold point (E) across to meet point (F).

13

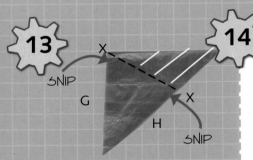

Cut off the triangle of plastic at the top, so that sides G and H are equal in length. Make a small snip at each of the corners marked (X).

14

Open out the plastic shape. This is the canopy of the parachute. Use scissors to make a small hole 1 cm above each of the eight small slits.

15

Measure the distance across the diameter of the parachute and cut eight pieces of string to that length.
Take one length of string and fold back 10 cm, creating a loop. Push the looped end through the hole in the plastic.

16

Feed the loose ends of the string through the loop. Pull tight. Repeat with the other seven pieces of string.

17

Cut small pieces of duct tape and stick a piece of tape over the front and back of each hole, enclosing the string.

18 Fold the parachute in half. Then into quarters, eighths and sixteenths (see pictures a–d).

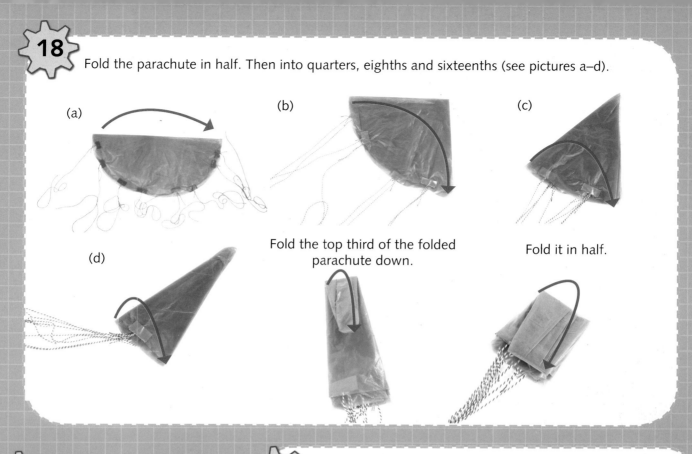

(a)

(b)

(c)

(d)

Fold the top third of the folded parachute down.

Fold it in half.

19

Gather the ends of the parachute strings together and tape them inside the end of the bottle rocket, using duct tape.

20 Take the 1-m length of string and use pieces of duct tape to stick one end to the nose cone you made in steps 6–8. Stick the other end inside the bottle rocket.

Push the folded plastic parachute inside the bottle.

21 Slide the nose cone onto the rocket.

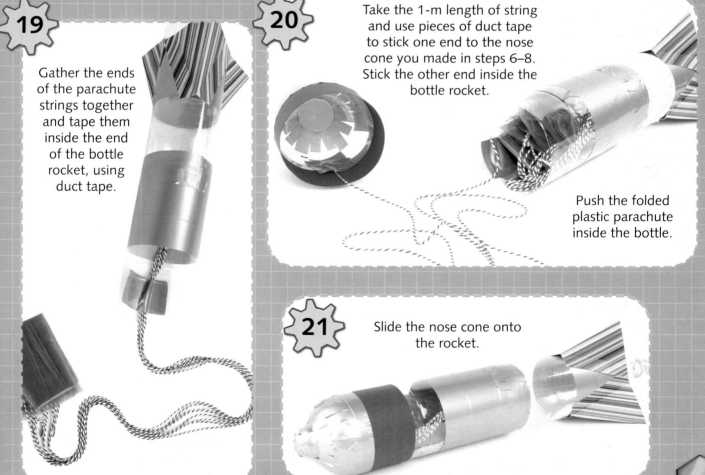

22

Ask an adult to make a hole through the cork large enough to fit the bicycle inner tube valve. Trim the cork so that the valve fits right through it and the cork fits the bottle rocket opening. Remove the cork and add water to the rocket until it is a quarter full. Replace the cork and set to one side.

To launch the super water rocket you will need:

- safety goggles
- drainage hopper (available from a builders' merchant or DIY store)
- measuring tape or ruler
- duct tape
- scissors
- circle of thick cardboard (same diameter as the inside of the hopper)
- piece of sponge or foam cut to fit inside the hopper
- 2 x pieces of wood, 20 cm longer than the length of the hopper and at least 10 cm deep
- 4 x hoop-shaped metal pegs (available from DIY stores)
- 4 x metal tent pegs

23

24

Cut a circle of card to fit the round part of the drainage hopper. Cut a hole in the centre of the cardboard circle a fraction bigger than the diameter of the cork that you fitted inside the super water rocket (see step 22 above). Push the cardboard into the hopper from the top so that the super water rocket will have a flat platform to stand on.

Tape the cardboard securely, using duct tape.

25

Cut a hole in the centre of the sponge or foam, a fraction bigger than the diameter of the cork. Gently push the circle of sponge down inside the hopper on top of the cardboard circle.

SAFETY FIRST

Wear safety goggles and always launch rockets outdoors. A rocket launch pad must be stable to ensure that the rocket will launch in the correct direction. A rocket that falls over during the launch is VERY dangerous.
Before you launch the rocket, read the safety code
on page 26.

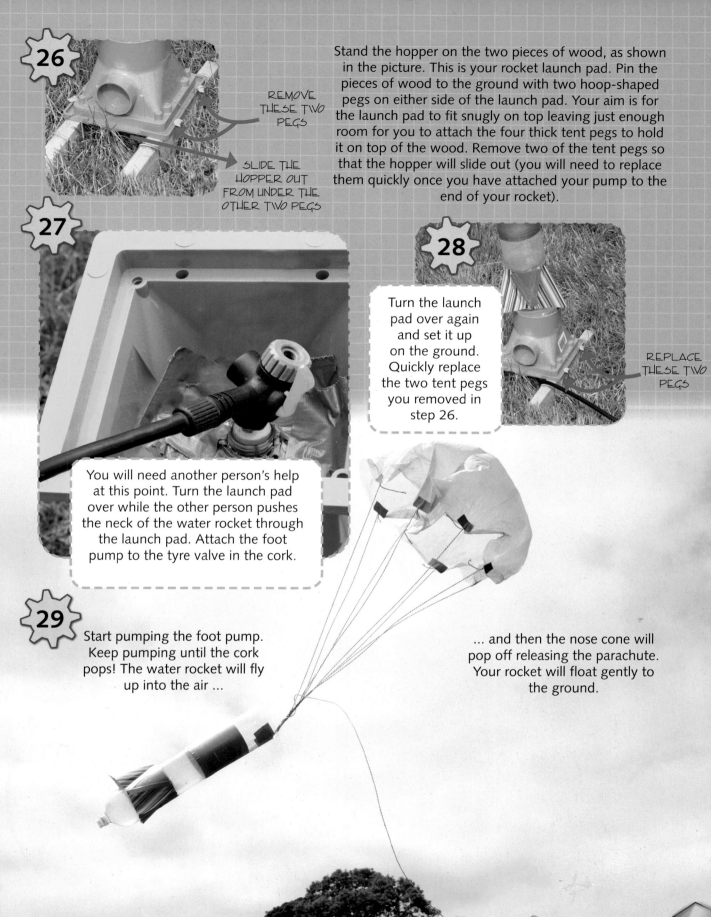

26 REMOVE THESE TWO PEGS

SLIDE THE HOPPER OUT FROM UNDER THE OTHER TWO PEGS

Stand the hopper on the two pieces of wood, as shown in the picture. This is your rocket launch pad. Pin the pieces of wood to the ground with two hoop-shaped pegs on either side of the launch pad. Your aim is for the launch pad to fit snugly on top leaving just enough room for you to attach the four thick tent pegs to hold it on top of the wood. Remove two of the tent pegs so that the hopper will slide out (you will need to replace them quickly once you have attached your pump to the end of your rocket).

27

28 Turn the launch pad over again and set it up on the ground. Quickly replace the two tent pegs you removed in step 26.

REPLACE THESE TWO PEGS

You will need another person's help at this point. Turn the launch pad over while the other person pushes the neck of the water rocket through the launch pad. Attach the foot pump to the tyre valve in the cork.

29 Start pumping the foot pump. Keep pumping until the cork pops! The water rocket will fly up into the air ...

... and then the nose cone will pop off releasing the parachute. Your rocket will float gently to the ground.

Tube rocket

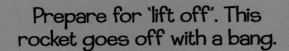

Prepare for 'lift off'. This rocket goes off with a bang.

How does it work? When the propellant in this model rocket engine ignites, it expels high pressure exhaust fumes from the base of the rocket. This produces thrust in the opposite direction which makes the tube rocket lift off.

Igniters

Model rocket igniters are small devices that allow you to launch a model rocket from a distance. When you attach the battery to the igniters, the igniters heat up. The heat makes the propellant in the rocket motor ignite (burn) and the rocket will shoot upwards from the launch pad.

To make the tube rocket you will need:

- cylinder of balsa wood, 2 cm x 8 cm
- sandpaper • small screw eye
- red paint • paintbrush
- 1 m length of thin cord
- stiff cardboard tube with 23 mm diameter (from a roll of cling film or aluminium foil)
- lightweight plastic bag
- scissors • masking tape
- hole punch • ruler
- coloured sticky tape
- drinking straw
- 3 x sheets of model rocket wadding (available from model rocket suppliers, see p. 32)
- D12-7 model rocket motor, 23 mm in diameter (including igniters and igniter plug, available from suppliers, see p. 32)

1

Use the sandpaper to shape the block of balsa wood to form the rocket nose cone. The flat end needs to fit snugly into the top of the cardboard tube. Screw the screw eye into the flat end of the balsa wood.

2 Paint the balsa wood red. Leave to dry. Knot the length of thin cord to the screw eye.

3 MASKING TAPE

Cut a strip of plastic, 60 cm by 7 cm, from a plastic bag. Stick a 7-cm length of masking tape along the 7-cm edge of the plastic strip. Punch a hole in the centre of the masking tape.

4

Fold the thin cord back on itself, 20 cm along from where it is tied to the screw eye. Push the loop of cord through the hole in the masking tape. Feed the loose ends of the cord and the nose cone through the loop. Pull tight.

5

Tape the cord in place with another piece of masking tape.

6

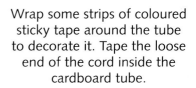

Wrap some strips of coloured sticky tape around the tube to decorate it. Tape the loose end of the cord inside the cardboard tube.

7

Roll up the strip of plastic. Push the rolled up plastic into the end of the tube where the cord is attached, followed by the cord and the balsa wood nose cone to form the tube rocket.

8

Tape the drinking straw to the side of the tube rocket level with the opposite end to the nose cone.

9

Push the sheets of model rocket wadding into the bottom of the tube rocket.

10

Push the model rocket motor into the base of the tube rocket, leaving 1 cm sticking out of the end. Tape in place with masking tape.

11

Place the igniters inside the hole, leaving the two metal connectors sticking out. Push in the plastic igniter plug.

To launch the tube rocket you will need:
(For the launch pad)
- pencil
- ruler
- piece of wood, 50 cm x 30 cm x 3 cm
- piece of wood, 10 cm x 10 cm x 3 cm
- piece of straightened coathanger wire, 1 m long (it is very important that the wire is straight)
- drill, with a drill bit the same size as the diameter of the wire
- wood glue and spreader
- duct tape.
- bottle top to cap the wire when not in use

(To launch the rocket)
- safety goggles
- tube rocket launch pad (see above)
- 9V battery
- crocodile clips • electrical tape
- 2 x 10 m lengths of speaker wire
(last three items available from electrical stores, see p. 32)

12

Use the pencil and ruler to draw diagonal lines from corner to corner of the larger piece of wood. Repeat for the smaller piece of wood. Place the small piece of wood on top of the larger piece of wood, where the pencil lines cross. Stick it down firmly using wood glue. Leave to dry.
Ask an adult to drill through both pieces of wood where the lines cross in the centre.

13

Tape the small piece of wood to the large piece of wood with duct tape. Leave a space around the central hole.
Thread the coathanger wire through the hole.

14

Bend 1 cm of wire at a right angle under the piece of wood to keep it in place. Tape it in position. Set the launch pad upright. The wire must be straight and vertical.

15 Put the bottle cap on top of the wire whenever you do not have the rocket in place. This is to prevent an eye injury.

16 Remove the cap from the wire. Place the rocket on the launch pad with the wire through the drinking straw attached to the side of the rocket. This will help the rocket to fly straight up into the air.

17 Attach the crocodile clips to the small wires at the base of the rocket.
Lay the speaker wires along the ground in a straight line away from the rocket.

SAFETY FIRST
Clear the launch area.

Follow the manufacturer's instructions for attaching the battery to launch the rocket motor you have chosen. Ensure you follow all the safety instructions given by them as well as those included in our safety code for more advanced rockets (see page 27).

18 Count down: 5, 4, 3, 2, 1 ...
Attach the battery. The rocket will blast off into the sky with the streamer unfolding behind it.

Model Rocket Safety Code

For water rockets:

Safety is very important when you are launching a rocket, however small or light. Water rockets are NOT toys. A pressurised water rocket stores huge amounts of energy and flies very fast. THEY CAN BURST!

Children should never launch water rockets without adult supervision.

Only plastic, fizzy (carbonated) drink bottles should be used. DO NOT use bottles made for non-fizzy drinks, such as still water.

Only use lightweight materials to build your rocket, such as paper, wood, rubber and plastic.
DO NOT USE METAL FOR ANY PART OF YOUR ROCKET.

Never use your water rocket to carry live animals or any payload that is intended to be flammable, explosive or harmful and only fill it with water.

Never over pressurise your bottle – no more than 90 pounds per square inch, which is also written as 90 psi (metric: 620.5 kPa.) Use a good quality pump with a pressure gauge to show pressure when launching.

Launch your water rocket from a stable device.

Make sure you only launch your rocket outdoors in a cleared area, free from tall trees, power lines and buildings.

Make sure that anyone watching is at least 5 m from the water rocket during launch and behind the person launching it.

IT IS YOUR RESPONSIBILITY TO ENSURE THAT PEOPLE IN THE LAUNCH AREA ARE AWARE THAT A LAUNCH IS ABOUT TO TAKE PLACE.

YOU MUST GIVE AT LEAST A FIVE SECOND COUNTDOWN.

DO NOT ALLOW ANYONE TO PUT THEIR HEAD OR ANY OTHER PART OF THEIR BODY ABOVE THE ROCKET DURING OR AFTER PRESSURISATION.

Remember – even if you do not have a successful launch, the water rocket may still blast off when you touch it.

Do not aim your water rocket at anyone or anything.

Do not launch in windy conditions.

RETIRE YOUR ROCKET AFTER 10 to 15 LAUNCHES.

For more advanced rockets
(Tube rocket pages 22–25)

If you are launching more advanced rockets you must follow the code for launching water rockets, opposite, but also follow this additional set of safety rules.

Only use certified, commercially made rocket motors and ensure they are not tampered with. Read the manufacturer's instructions.

If the rocket does not launch, disconnect the battery and wait at least 60 seconds before allowing anyone to approach the rocket.

Rockets must be launched from a launch rod, tower or rail that is pointed to within 30 degrees of the vertical to ensure that the rocket flies straight up.

The launch rod must be above eye level – or be capped when not in use.

Only use flame-proof wadding in your rocket.

Always launch rockets outdoors.

Make sure that weather conditions are suitable and that there is no dry grass close to the launch pad that could catch light.

Templates

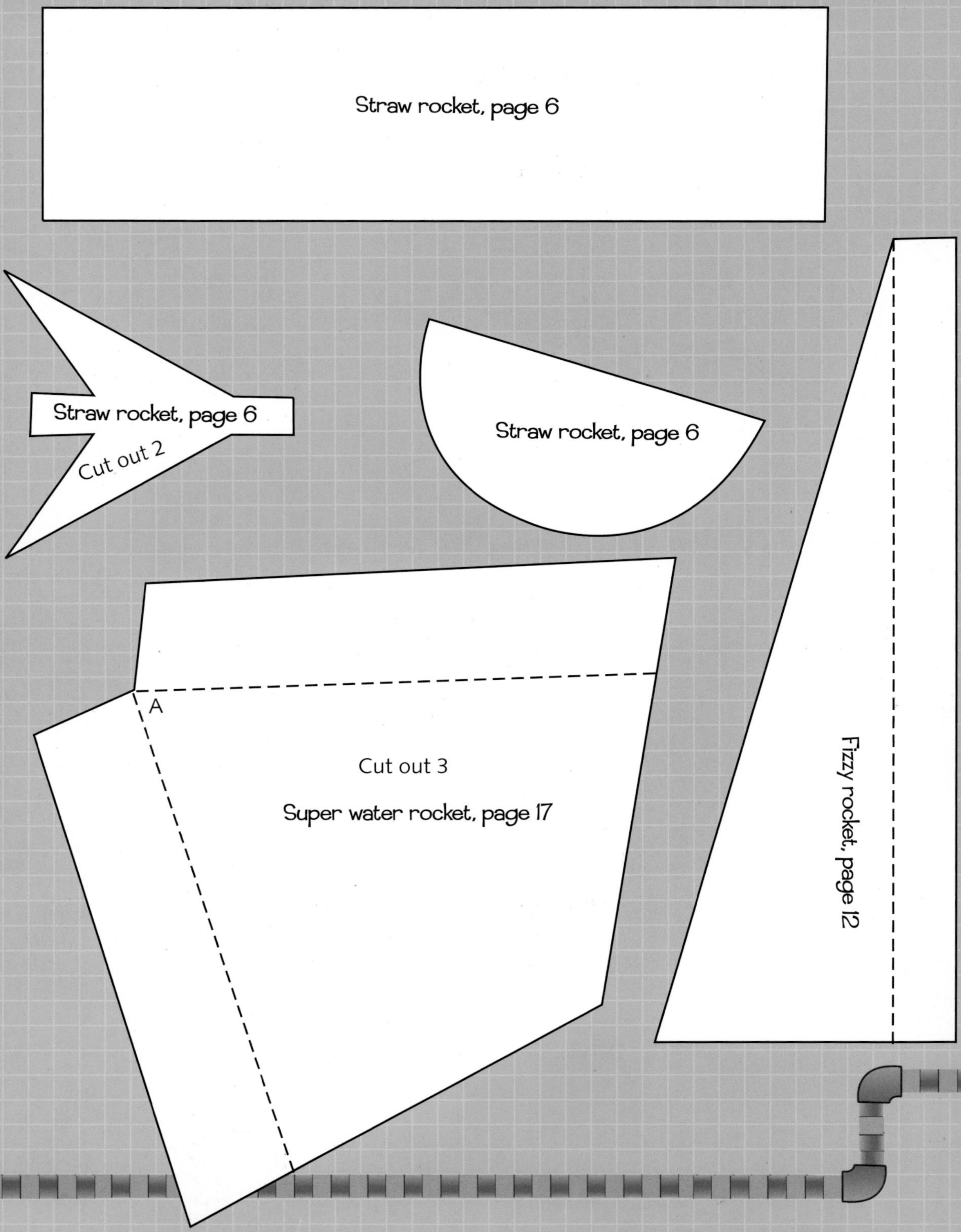

Straw rocket, page 6

Straw rocket, page 6

Cut out 2

Straw rocket, page 6

Cut out 3

Super water rocket, page 17

A

Fizzy rocket, page 12

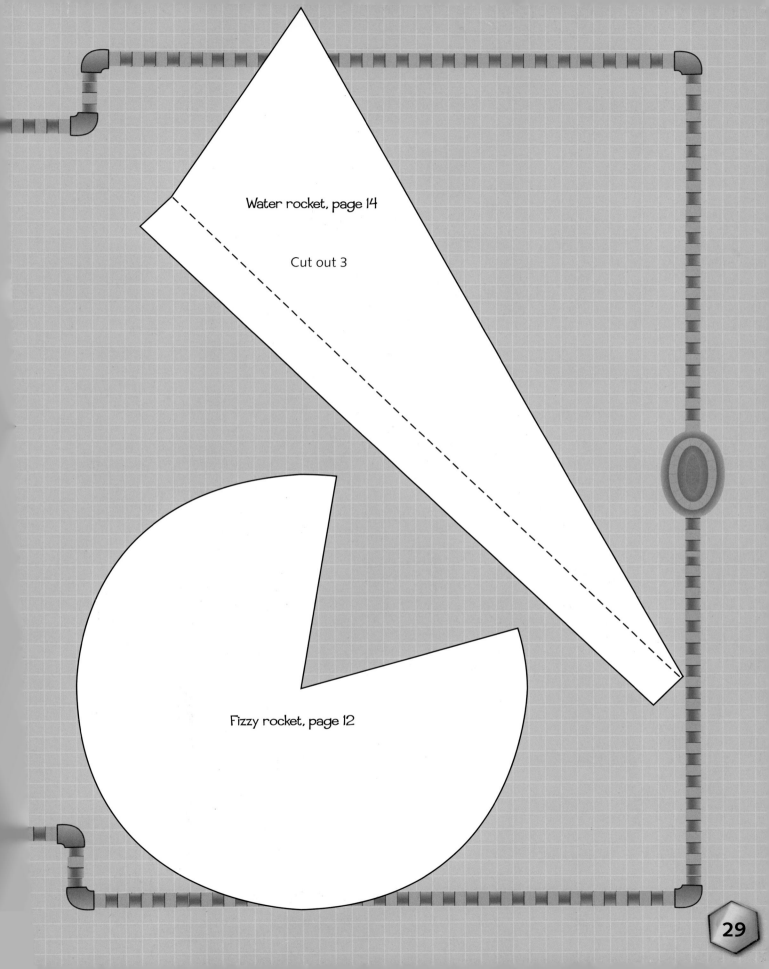

Water rocket, page 14

Cut out 3

Fizzy rocket, page 12

29

Rockets timeline

The Chinese invented an early form of gunpowder. They filled bamboo tubes with gunpowder, attached them to arrows and launched them using bows.

1200s

1687

The British scientist, Sir Isaac Newton (1642–1727), published his Laws of Motion.

In Britain, Colonel William Congreve (1772–1828) developed a rocket that reached a height of almost 5.5 km. The Congreve rocket was used by the Royal Navy in the 1812 war against the United States of America.

1804

American engineer and inventor, Dr Robert Goddard (1882–1945), launched the world's first liquid-fuelled rocket. Goddard was convinced a rocket could reach the Moon and spent his life trying to develop ways to make this possible. At the time he did not receive much support for his work but after his death he became known as 'the father of modern rocketry'.

1926

A team of German scientists led by Wernher von Braun developed the V-2, the first rocket capable of reaching space. The rocket was an unmanned, guided, ballistic missile fuelled by alcohol and liquid oxygen. It had a range of 320 km and could travel at an altitude of 88.5 km. Carrying an explosive warhead, it brought terror to the people of France and Britain in the last year of the Second World War (1939–1945).

1942

1957

The Soviet Union launched *Sputnik 1* in October 1957, the first satellite to orbit the Earth. Two months later, *Sputnik II* carried Laika, a dog, into space.

1961

On 20 July, the *Apollo 11* space mission, using the powerful Saturn V rocket, landed American astronauts Neil Armstrong and Buzz Aldrin on the Moon.

1969

Soviet cosmonaut, Yuri Gagarin, was the first human in space. On 12 April he orbited Earth once inside *Vostok I* in a flight that lasted one hour and 48 minutes.

1998

The International Space Station (ISS), a joint project funded by five international space agencies, launched its first stage.

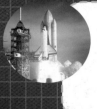

NASA launched its first space shuttle in 1981. Space shuttles were reusable vehicles used to carry satellites, telescopes, space probes and other equipment into space. The last space shuttle mission occurred in 2011.

1981–2011

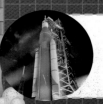

The future
NASA is testing new rockets that will make it possible to explore much further into space than ever before.

Glossary

Airtight Not allowing air to pass through.

Altitude Height above sea level.

Ballistic missile A missile (rocket) that shoots into the sky, follows an arching pathway, and then falls to Earth, where its warheads explode.

Drag A force that pulls back on a moving object.

Energy Energy is the ability to do work and it comes in several forms including heat, light, chemical energy and electricity.

Force A push or a pull.

Friction A force that slows down movement when one surface slides over another.

Gravity A force of attraction between all objects. Earth's gravity pulls everything towards the ground.

Lift The upward force produced on a wing when it moves through the air.

Orbit The path of a spacecraft or planet around a star or planet.

Payload The equipment, passengers or cargo carried by a rocket.

Pressure How much force is concentrated on a particular area.

Propellant A substance that is able to propel something. In firework rockets the propellant is gunpowder and in space rockets it is rocket fuel.

Recovery When stages of space rockets are recovered, the authorities locate them, collect them and bring them back to the space centre.

Thrust A pushing force that moves something forward.

Warhead Explosive material delivered by a rocket.

Further information

The NASA website is a brilliant source of information about space rockets. Find out about its new Space Launch System that will send astronauts further into our solar system than ever before:

http://www.nasa.gov/exploration/systems/sls/index.html

Build a virtual rocket:

http://www.nasa.gov/externalflash/RocketScience101/
RocketScience101.html

Watch and listen to clips from BBC broadcasts relating to space missions:

www.bbc.co.uk/science/space/solarsystem/space_missions

Index

Crafts and parts suppliers

Craft shops, art shops, office suppliers and stationery shops will sell most of the materials you will need to build the models in this book – and you will be able to use materials you have at home or at school.

A good online craft store is: www.bakerross.co.uk

This electronics supplier sells electric motors and other related components: www.maplin.co.uk

Rocket motors are available online from online suppliers including:
http://www.rapidonline.com
http://hurricanemodels.co.uk

Note to parents and teachers: every effort has been made by the Publishers to ensure that these websites are suitable for children, that they are of the highest educational value, and that they contain no inappropriate or offensive material. However, because of the nature of the Internet, it is impossible to guarantee that the contents of these sites will not be altered. We strongly advise that Internet access is supervised by a responsible adult.